THE 10™

Most Fascinating Phenomena

Sunniva Buskermolen

Series Editor
Jeffrey D. Wilhelm

Much thought, debate, and research went into choosing and ranking the 10 items in each book in this series. We realize that everyone has his or her own opinion of what is most significant, revolutionary, amazing, deadly, and so on. As you read, you may agree with our choices, or you may be surprised — and that's the way it should be!

Franklin Watts
an imprint of
SCHOLASTIC
www.scholastic.com/librarypublishing

A Rubicon book published in association with Scholastic Inc.

Rubicon © 2007 Rubicon Publishing Inc.
www.rubiconpublishing.com

Associate Publishers: Kim Koh, Miriam Bardswich
Project Editor: Amy Land
Editor: Joyce Thian
Creative Director: Jennifer Drew
Project Manager/Designer: Jeanette MacLean
Graphic Designer: Rebecca Buchanan

The publisher gratefully acknowledges the following for permission to reprint copyrighted material in this book.

Every reasonable effort has been made to trace the owners of copyrighted material and to make due acknowledgment. Any errors or omissions drawn to our attention will be gladly rectified in future editions.

"Vesuvius shows signs of another big bang" (excerpt) by Robert Matthews. From *The Telegraph*. April 12, 1998. © Telegraph Media Group Ltd.

"Exploding Star May Produce Backyard Show" (excerpt) by Robert Roy Britt. From SPACE.com, January 7, 2003. Found at http://www.space.com/scienceastronomy/exploding_star_030107.html. © 1999–2007 Imaginova Corp. All rights reserved. Reprinted with permission.

Cover image: Comet–Getty Images/10024814/Kauko Helavuo

Library and Archives Canada Cataloguing in Publication

Buskermolen, Sunniva
      The 10 most fascinating phenomena/Sunniva Buskermolen.

Includes index.
ISBN 978-1-55448-471-3

      1. Readers (Elementary) 2. Readers — Curiosities and wonders
I. Title. II. Title: Ten most fascinating phenomena.

PE1117.B98 2007   428.6   C2007-900543-8

1 2 3 4 5 6 7 8 9 10   10   16 15 14 13 12 11 10 09 08 07

Printed in Singapore

Contents

14

22

38

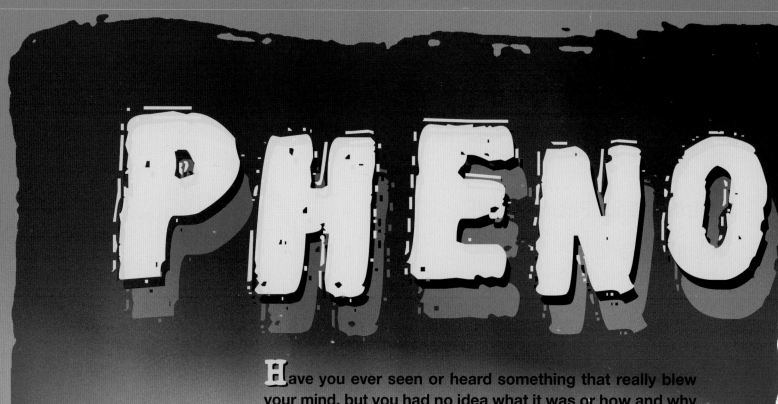

PHENO

Have you ever seen or heard something that really blew your mind, but you had no idea what it was or how and why it happened?

Phenomena are unusual, significant, and sometimes unaccountable events in nature that can be felt by the senses. In this book, we'll travel through deserts, oceans, and even to the far reaches of space to bring you 10 of the most fascinating phenomena in the universe. These naturally occurring events amaze and puzzle even the smartest scientists. Many of these phenomena are so rare that only a handful of people on Earth have ever seen them. In fact, some of the phenomena are still unexplained mysteries — even the experts can't agree on exactly what's going on.

The phenomena that appear in this book are all being actively researched by astronomers, physicists, biologists, oceanographers, and geologists.

It was difficult, but we made our list and ranked the phenomena according to these criteria: their rarity; their power and magnitude; their impact on the surrounding environment, humans, and other living creatures; and their extraordinary or even unaccountable causes.

MENAL!

Based on these criteria, what do you think is the most **fascinating phenomenon in the world?**

10 SINGING SA

The sand dunes
of the Gobi Desert
are known for their
booming sand concerts.

WHAT IS IT? Sand that squeaks or booms when it moves

WOW FACTOR: Booming sand can be as loud as 115 decibels (imagine standing six feet away from a running chainsaw or jackhammer).

Welcome to the most unusual concert of your life. And the headlining act is ... sand!

For centuries, explorers and scientists around the world have described strange sounds coming from sand dunes in deserts. Sound-producing dunes were described in Chinese and Middle Eastern literature more than 1,500 years ago. Even the famous traveler Marco Polo made a note of these sand symphonies in his travel book. He thought it was the musical work of evil desert spirits!

Scientists today have a better explanation, but even they admit they're still stumped. Read on to find out more about the fascinating phenomenon known as singing sand. It kicks off our list at #10 ...

Go online to find a sound clip of singing sand. How would you describe this singing? Would you call this music or just plain noise? What's the difference?

SINGING SAND

WHAT ABOUT IT?

There are two kinds of singing sand — "booming" and "squeaking." Booming sand produces a loud and low sound, like a plane flying really low or a foghorn. It can last for many minutes. Squeaking sand produces more of a mini concert of squeaks or whistles.

BUT HOW?

Booming sand is produced during a "sand-slide" (a sand avalanche) in a desert dune. Squeaking sand is produced when you step on or cut your way through the sand on a beach. In other words, some sort of movement is required to produce any sort of singing. Beyond that, not even the scientists who study singing sand know exactly how this phenomenon works.

WHERE IN THE WORLD?

Booming sand dunes have been heard in 30 locations worldwide, including North and South America, Africa, Asia, the Middle East, and the Hawaiian Islands. Squeaking sand can be heard on certain beaches. There's one catch — singing sand will sing only if it's pure and dry. So with air and sea pollution on the rise around the world, some scientists are concerned that the singing sand phenomenon could soon disappear!

? Do you think you could produce sounds from the sand found in a nearby park in your neighborhood? Why or why not? Give it a try to test it out!

Quick Fact

Some scientists think that the planet Mars may actually be host to sand concerts too. It has the perfect conditions — it's super dry and windy and has just enough of an atmosphere for sound waves.

BOOMING!

squeaking

The Expert Says...

"When you bring a new team out to the Gobi [Desert] for the first time, among the other things they're amazed and disoriented by are the sounds of the sand. It's a remarkable sound."

— Michael Novacek, curator, American Museum of Natural History

10 9 8 7 6

Musical Mystery

Scientists conduct different experiments to try to find explanations for various phenomena. Check out this fact chart to find out what some scientists have discovered about singing sand!

Franco Nori and Michael Bretz, physicists, University of Michigan

In 1997, Nori and Bretz did a series of tests with singing sand. One of their discoveries was that adding just five drops of water to four liters of booming sand silenced it.

Stéphane Douady, physicist, French national research agency (CNRS)

In 2001, a research team led by Douady discovered that they could make singing sand sing just by pushing it around. He concluded that singing dunes boom due to the motion of the sand grains themselves, and not because the entire dune resonates. Later, he even created an experiment where he could produce any musical note he wanted, by moving the sand at different speeds in a controlled way.

Marcel Leach and Douglas Goldsack, physicists, Laurentian University

In 1997, Leach and Goldsack discovered there was a thin coating of silica gel on grains of singing sands. They wondered whether this silica gel might have anything to do with the singing phenomenon. So they bought some manufactured silica gel grains, put them in a jar, and shook it. Sure enough, the grains hummed! Though they couldn't say for sure that sand sings because of silica gel, they could now at least conclude that silica gel had something to do with it.

silica gel: solid and colorless chemical compound

Take Note

Singing sand kicks off our list of fascinating phenomena at #10 because it puts on such a good show. Even though it doesn't seem to have an impact on the environment, it's still a fascinating phenomenon for scientists who are trying to figure out what causes it.

- Do your own research to find other theories about the cause of singing sand. Why do you think different scientists come up with different explanations for unexplained phenomena?

5   4   3   2   1

9 MIRAGE

Don't be fooled! What looks like a giant pool of water here in the Namib Desert, Namibia, is just another typical mirage.

WHAT IS IT? An optical trick of nature that occurs when light rays bend

WOW FACTOR: All it takes is a slight change in temperature (either a drop or a rise of about 5 degrees Fahrenheit) for a mirage to form.

"Water! Water!" You've probably heard the tale of the parched desert traveler. The traveler sees a shimmering pool of liquid salvation off in the distance and thinks, "An oasis, finally!" But what's there one minute is gone the next …

Desperate desert crossers aren't the only ones who get fooled by strange visions. On hot days, drivers see shimmering pools on otherwise dry roads; explorers see ships sailing upside down; and many UFO believers are convinced they've seen spaceships in the sky. No, they're not all imagining things. They have each been tricked by the optical phenomenon of the mirage.

Before modern navigational instruments were invented, travelers could become confused and lost because of what they thought they saw. Don't make the same mistake they did — read on to discover more about this fascinating phenomenon at #9 on our list …

optical: relating to sight; visual

 Have you ever been fooled by a mirage? At what point did you realize it was a mirage?

MIRAGE

WHAT ABOUT IT?

Mirages aren't illusions, they're not imaginary — they're real images (which you can actually photograph)! Objects appear out of place and distorted.

BUT HOW?

First off, we see an object because light rays are bouncing off it and into our eyes. Light rays usually travel through the air in straight lines. But when they hit hot air, they bend slightly (called refraction). The refracted rays of light basically move or shift the image of an object from its true location.

Quick Fact

In the past, desert travelers who reported seeing mirages were told they had only tricked themselves into seeing ponds in the desert, because they were so desperate to find water.

This mirage of a floating island in front of the setting sun is called a "looming" mirage. Here, the air above the water was cooler than the air higher up, which created the reverse mirage.

WHERE IN THE WORLD?

Mirages can be seen wherever there's a flat surface, where the air above it can get heated up in layers. Drivers often see pools of water on the road, because road surfaces are often flat and paved with material that can easily heat up during the day. Large-scale looming mirages (see photo above) are most common over the ocean or in polar regions, especially over large ice sheets.

 How can mirages affect people in their everyday lives? Think of who could be affected.

The Expert Says...

"Mirages make it difficult to identify land features during the day. If mirages are occurring ... plan your routes of travel at dawn or dusk or during moonlight hours."

— Gregory J. Davenport, author of *Surviving the Desert*

It looks like there is water on the road, but the pavement is completely dry. The "pool" is just a mirage of the sky!

STOPPED IN THEIR TRACKS

A recurring mirage stopped at least three teams of explorers from traveling through a channel in the Arctic waters. Read about their experiences in this timeline.

1818 A seafaring expedition sets out from Britain for North America. Explorers John and James Ross are looking to find the Northwest Passage, a legendary channel that explorers were sure connected the Atlantic and Pacific Oceans. They sail into the Arctic waters between Greenland and Baffin Bay. But their way is blocked by a range of mountains looming ahead of them. Forced to turn back, they report that the Northwest Passage does not exist.

1893 Explorer Robert Peary arrives at the same point where the Ross expedition stopped in 1818. He sees the same obstacle in the waters and also decides the route is blocked. He calls the range of mountains Crocker Land and heads elsewhere to search for the Northwest Passage.

1913 An expedition led by Donald MacMillan sets out to explore Crocker Land. They find the mountains — about 185 miles west of the position reported by the previous explorers. As they continue on, the mountains seem to retreat right before their eyes! Then, as the sun begins to set, the explorers are astonished by another weird sight: the mountain peaks of Crocker Land suddenly disappear into thin air! They realize the mountains that stopped John and James Ross and Robert Peary weren't mountains at all. They were just mirages all along!

? What would you have done if you had been in the same situation as the Rosses or Peary? Would you have turned back or kept going?

Take Note

Even though singing sand at #10 is a rarer occurrence than mirages, it doesn't have as great an effect on human activity. Mirages, on the other hand, have confused and misled countless travelers and explorers.
- Mirages are common sights today. Why is that? Think of changes humans have made to the landscape.

8 TIDAL BORE

Watching a tidal bore come in can be a dangerous activity. This one took place on the Qiantang River in Hangzhou, China.

For many people, waves coming in at a beach or rocky coast are a great source of wonder. The rhythmic pattern of the tides and the power of the rolling ocean can be mesmerizing things to watch.

In some parts of the world, though, these tides can bring an unexpected surprise. When tides come inland in certain areas, they can cause a striking phenomenon known as the tidal bore. The most famous of all tidal bores is the one that regularly churns up the Qiantang River in Hangzhou, China. It has reached heights of around 30 feet and speeds of 25 miles an hour!

The tidal bore rushes into the #8 spot on our list …

mesmerizing: *fascinating*

TIDAL BORE

WHAT ABOUT IT?

Tidal bores are tidal waves that rush upstream from an ocean into a river. They can be churning and tumbling walls of water, or they can be rolling and smooth ripples.

The Expert Says...

"The impact on the ecology is acknowledged in the Amazon where piranhas eat matter in suspension after the passage of the bore ...

— H. Chanson, professor, Department of Civil Engineering, University of Queensland

acknowledged: *recognized*
suspension: *floating state*

? Tidal bores have sometimes been mistaken for another wave phenomenon: the tsunami. Do some research on tsunamis. How can you tell the difference between the two phenomena?

BUT HOW?

Tidal bores occur only in areas where there is a large tidal range (meaning, there's a big height difference between high and low tides), as well as a V-shaped bay. In these places, when the tide comes inland, the shores of the bay funnel large amounts of water toward the mouth of a river. The tide then forms into a tidal bore as it begins rushing up the river, which still flows in the opposite direction. Rivers become narrower and shallower as they continue inland, so the bore gets squeezed upward. This creates a piling effect, turning the bore into a tall, rushing wave. The tidal bore continues to flow up the river until the energy of the original wave is used up.

WHERE IN THE WORLD?

Tidal bores have been spotted in about 100 places in the world. It's very rare to find both conditions needed to create a bore. Big and powerful bores can be found in parts of South and Southeast Asia, Australia, the United Kingdom, Canada, and Brazil.

HOW TIDAL BORES FORM

Quick Fact

Tides are caused by the gravitational attraction of the sun and moon on Earth's waters.

River
River flow
Tidal bore
Land
Tidal wave
Ocean

Note: The depth and width of the river increase in the direction of its flow — creating a funnel.

A Brazilian surfer catches the thunderous pororoca tidal bore on the Mearim River in Brazil. Pororoca means "destroyer, great blast."

Surfing the Bore

A growing number of extreme sport enthusiasts have made surfing tidal bores their new pastime. Unlike regular surfing, which lasts for only as long as a wave can sustain itself, this new sport allows a surfer to ride a single wave upstream for miles and minutes on end. Though this sport isn't for everyone, you can read these quotations for an idea of what it's like to try to surf a bore!

"The wave is very powerful and can destroy anything — trees, local houses, islands … and sweeps up wild animals, like snakes — the anaconda — alligators, spiders, piranha, and even jaguars."

— Serginho Laus, professional surfer, describing the tidal bores in Brazil

"In the thick of the rapids, it was like riding a bucking bronco, with one hand grasping the rope along the raft gunwale and the other swinging wildly, while buckets of water are thrown at you."

— Peter Leney, describing a trip up the Shubenacadie River in the Bay of Fundy in Canada

gunwale: *upper edge of a boat's side*

"You could hear the noise, like a steam train hurtling round the corner. And, around the corner, we were met by a 5-foot solid head of water which was getting bigger and bigger. By the time it got to Garden Cliff, it was at least 9 feet — almost double overhead."

— Steve King, professional surfer, describing the bore that travels up Britain's longest river

Take Note

Not only are tidal bores striking events to watch, but they can also be very powerful and therefore dangerous to people in the surrounding area. This is why they come in at #8, above the mirage at #9, which does not have a direct effect on people or on the environment surrounding it.
• What do you think scientists look out for when studying tidal bores? Think of how tidal bores change the environment.

5   4   3   2   1

⑦ QUICKSAND

As this character in a 1961 movie discovers, the more you struggle, the faster you'll sink in a pit of quicksand!

MAN IN QUICKSAND—© BETTMANN/CORBIS

WHAT IS IT? Soft, wet sand that's quick to swallow anything heavy that falls into it

WOW FACTOR: A panicking victim or an entire train engine can be buried within seconds!

For centuries, people believed that quicksand had some kind of strange suction power. One wrong step and the killer sandpit would suck you down into the ground, swallowing you whole. Naturally, with this sort of reputation, quicksand terrified most people.

But chalk this one up to misinformation — quicksand isn't as dramatic as old Hollywood movies presented it to be. We now know that people who are "killed" by quicksand usually die from being drowned by an incoming tide or from exhaustion and exposure. Death hardly ever comes from being "sucked" in by a pit of quicksand.

All the same, quicksand is still regarded as a powerful phenomenon of nature. One minute it looks like a solid (but acts like a liquid); the next minute it looks like a liquid (but acts like a solid)! Confused? Read on to find out what the deal is with our #7 phenomenon …

QUICKSAND

WHAT ABOUT IT?

Quicksand is really just regular sand that's floating loosely on underground water lying just beneath the surface. Sometimes, mud and vegetation may also be mixed into the sand, giving it a thick, soupy consistency that can be very sticky.

BUT HOW?

Some form of movement is needed to actually make the sand "quick." For example, something falls into the pit, disturbing the delicate balancing act of the floating sand. At this point, the sand collapses and begins to mix with the water, and the whole sandpit turns into soupy quicksand. The water lifts and separates each tiny grain of sand so that the mixture acts like a liquid (though it feels more like sludge).

Even strong and tough vehicles can get stuck in quicksand.

WHERE IN THE WORLD?

Quicksand can form almost anywhere under the right conditions. You're most likely to find quicksand near marshes and bogs, riverbeds or streambeds, valleys, riverbanks, beaches, and underground springs. Quicksand can also form when an earthquake loosens sand and silt deposits. For example, in 1964, apartment buildings in Niigata, Japan, tipped over like dominoes after an earthquake. The ground had liquefied into a kind of quicksand and could no longer support the weight of the buildings.

 What types of human activity might lead to more occurrences of quicksand?

DANGER SINKING MUD

A sign warning of quicksand on a beach in England

 **Quick Fact**

Some of the best preserved bones from dinosaurs and other prehistoric creatures are from those that got caught in quicksand. Stuck in the sandpit, their remains were well protected from weather damage and scavengers.

The Expert Says...

"Quicksand is an unstable soil that you sink away in when walking on. ... The sand grains are piled up so loosely that quicksand liquefies when made to flow: this is why one shouldn't move when trapped in it. However, one should not panic: due to the buoyancy force, it is impossible to drown in quicksand."

— Dr. Daniel Bonn, physics professor, University of Amsterdam

buoyancy: *ability to stay afloat*

Getting Out Alive!

A scientist with the U.S. Geology Survey fell into quicksand while exploring the Colorado River. To get out, it took him eight hours to swim a 10-foot distance.

An encounter with quicksand doesn't need to end in disaster. Here's an instruction guide to getting out alive:

Don't panic!

Flailing or struggling will disturb the quicksand mixture even more than you already have. This will only dig you deeper into the liquid sandpit.

flailing: *wildly swinging one's arms and legs*

? In what other situations do things get worse when you panic? Why does panicking make things worse?

Relax ...

Believe it or not, you can actually float in quicksand, because your body is less dense than the sand. In fact, it's easier to float in quicksand than in water! The key is to relax and try to lie flat on your back, spreading your arms and legs far apart to increase your surface area.

Take it easy!

Once you've floated to the top of the sandpit, you can try to make your escape. Keep all your movements slow and gentle and start paddling to firm ground. Don't kick. This may take a long time, but you can eventually "swim" your way through and out of the sludge.

Drop it!

If you're carrying anything heavy, drop it right away. Having something to hold on to might feel safer, but it will only make you sink more in the end.

Don't force yourself!

The force needed to pull a panicking victim free from quicksand is equal to that needed to lift a small car! That's because the more you disturb the quicksand, the more it hardens like concrete.

Take Note

While tidal bores can be powerful, they are limited to a few specific areas in the world. Meanwhile, quicksand can occur pretty much anywhere with the right conditions. At the same time, its deceptive appearance can put unsuspecting passersby in serious danger! It takes our #7 spot.
• When was the last time you fell victim to a deceptive appearance? Give an example.

5   4   3   2   1

Locust swarms can be awfully scary, but at least they won't attack humans! They will, however, try to devour all our crops.

RM

WHAT IS IT? Locusts are usually solitary insects, but when they start gathering together in large numbers, they form huge roving swarms.

WOW FACTOR: Millions of locusts swarming together can destroy all vegetation in their path!

Have you ever seen a locust swarm? Just imagine millions upon millions of grasshopper-like insects flying together in a huge black cloud. As they approach, their flapping wings and colliding bodies make a sound that's like a powerful hailstorm.

Sound like something out of a horror movie? This sort of scene is all too real in certain parts of the world. Besides being a scary sight, locust swarms can completely destroy the areas they infest. A very small part of an average swarm (about one ton of locusts) can eat the same amount of food in one day as 10 elephants or 2,500 people! No wonder people have been comparing them to "plagues" since ancient times.

Read on to find out more about this amazing swarming phenomenon, including how and why it happens.

LOCUST SWARM

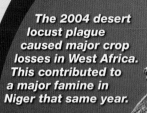

The 2004 desert locust plague caused major crop losses in West Africa. This contributed to a major famine in Niger that same year.

WHAT ABOUT IT?

The locust is a type of grasshopper that has big hind legs for jumping. When they swarm together, they can take up several hundred square miles of space. Within each square mile of a swarm, there can be anywhere from 15 to 30 million adult locusts. A swarm of locusts can migrate over large distances, covering 80 miles or more in a day! They usually fly with the wind, at a speed of up to 12 miles an hour.

BUT HOW?

Locust swarms occur when the right conditions, such as widespread rain and plant growth, allow locusts to breed in high numbers. When things get too crowded, the locusts bump up against one another — this is what triggers their swarming instincts! At the same time, they give off a pheromone that attracts other locusts — meaning a small gathering will turn into a large swarming. Scientists have discovered that at least 30 locusts are needed before they begin to gather in a bunch and start moving in the same direction.

pheromone: *chemical that influences the behavior of others of the same species*

WHERE IN THE WORLD?

Locust swarms occur in many parts of the world, including Africa, the Middle East, and Asia. Locusts can be found in over 60 countries. Today, the farming regions of Africa are the most hard-hit by locust plagues (the photograph in the background of this page shows a locust swarm in South Africa). These pesky locusts have the ability to threaten the economic livelihood of one-tenth of the world's humans!

? How can a locust plague in one area or country affect people in other parts of the world? Think about our global food supply.

The Expert Says...

" Locust swarms are among the most breathtaking — and mysterious — events in the natural world. "

— Dr. Jeffrey A. Lockwood, professor, Natural Sciences and Humanities, University of Wyoming

Quick Fact

Locusts and grasshoppers might look similar. But while locusts act differently in certain situations, grasshoppers just go about their own business no matter what changes around them.

10   **9**   **8**   **7**   **6**

COLLISION COURSE

When these insects migrate in dense swarms, how do they avoid crashing into each other? Read this report about the secret behind locusts' amazing navigational skills!

Locusts have a large neuron called the locust giant movement detector (LGMD). It's located behind the locust's eyes. It releases bursts of energy whenever a locust is on a collision course with another locust or a predatory bird. When something is coming directly at the locust, the neuron releases even more energy.

These sudden bursts of energy are called "action potentials" — they prompt the locust to take evasive action. It only takes a locust about 45 milliseconds — or 45 thousandths of a second — after the burst to get out of the way.

The locust can also see many more images per second than humans. Their view of the world is like us watching everything go by in slow motion.

neuron: *nerve cell that sends and receives electrical signals over long distances within the body*
evasive: *intended to get away from or avoid*

? Chemical insecticides can help control locust swarms, but they are also harmful to other living things. Is it acceptable to use this method to control a locust swarm? Consider the pros and cons.

Quick Fact

There are ways to kill locusts without using chemicals. Some methods use bacteria, fungi, algae, or viruses that produce a toxin harmful to the locust or cause a disease.

Take Note

As dangerous as quicksand is, you can avoid it if you're careful. But what about a locust swarm? There's not much you can do to stop it once it's on its way. Its sheer size and destructive power earn it the #6 spot.
• Why might scientists and farmers have different opinions about locust swarms?

5   4   3   2   1

5 AURORA

When an aurora appears near the North Pole, it's called aurora borealis (or northern lights). When it appears near the South Pole, it's called aurora australis (or southern lights).

WHAT IS IT? An incredible light show, most often seen near the North and South Poles

WOW FACTOR: A geomagnetic storm triggers this spectacular curtain of changing lights and colors — it moves and shimmers across the night sky.

An aurora is one of the most fascinating sights in the universe. It's a spectacular light show caused by none other than the mighty sun. Earth isn't the only planet that gets to see or experience this natural phenomenon. Scientists have found out that at least four other planets in our solar system — Jupiter, Saturn, Uranus, and Neptune — get auroras, too!

Best viewed on clear nights, auroras light up and electrify a dark sky. On February 11, 1958, the night sky over almost all of North America was clear, so millions of people, even those living as far south as Florida and southern California, saw a rare, completely blood-red aurora. It was so bright that it looked as if there was a huge fire burning in the distance. It even made the snow on the ground look red!

The fascinating aurora comes in at #5 on our list ...

AURORA

WHAT ABOUT IT?

An aurora can be many different colors, including white, yellow, green, red, blue, and violet. When viewed from space, auroras look like wide ovals centered on Earth's magnetic poles.

BUT HOW?

The process begins with eruptions on the surface of the sun. Solar flares send streams of electrically charged particles to Earth at high speeds. As these particles approach, Earth's magnetism pulls them in toward the North and South Poles. When they hit the upper atmosphere, they collide with oxygen and nitrogen atoms. Particles that collide with oxygen atoms react to produce a red and greenish-yellow glow. Particles that collide with nitrogen atoms glow blue and violet. This violent collision is called a geomagnetic storm.

WHERE IN THE WORLD?

Aurora activity is strongest during increased solar activity, which peaks about every 11 years. With intense geomagnetic storms, you can see a glimmer of the northern lights from as far south as Mexico. Since the polar regions experience 24-hour nights during the winter, these are excellent locations to view an aurora.

Quick Fact

Solar wind can reach speeds of 1.5 million miles an hour. It can carry away more than two billion pounds of charged particles from the sun every second.

?

Why do you think scientists study auroras? Think about what they can learn about solar flares, solar wind, and Earth's atmosphere.

Quick Fact

The electricity of the geomagnetic storms that produce auroras can directly disrupt electrical power, causing blackouts over large regions. The radiation these storms produce can also damage satellites, disturbing telephone, radio, and television signals.

Solar flare

The Expert Says...

"When we see auroral displays in the sky ... nature is projecting a picture of the sun's interaction with the Earth's extended magnetic field on our upper atmosphere. What a marvelous chance for us humans to see the forces of the universe. ..."

— Dr. Daniel Baker, professor and director, Laboratory for Atmospheric and Space Physics, University of Colorado

10   9   8   7   6

LEGENDARY AURORA

The aurora lights have been impressing people around the world for thousands of years. Before scientists figured out what really caused auroras, people came up with their own explanations for the spectacular light show. Here's a sample of the different legends about this seemingly inexplicable phenomenon:

In *Latvian* folklore, the northern lights were said to be the fighting souls of dead warriors. When they appeared, it was supposed to be a sign of an approaching disaster, like war or famine.

In East Asia, *Chinese* legends often portrayed the moving bands of active aurora lights as serpents, because they looked like twisting snakes in the sky.

The ALGONQUIN, a Native American people living along the Ottawa River in Canada, believed the lights to be their ancestors dancing around a ceremonial fire.

In the North American Arctic, *INUIT* folklore said that the dashing lights of an aurora signaled that dancing spirits were playing a ball game in the sky.

In Northern Europe, VIKING legends said that the polar lights were reflections from the shields of dead warriors rising into heaven.

Take Note

Compared to the previous five phenomena, the aurora can have a much more disruptive effect on humans and the surrounding environment. It's an energetic and visually stunning display of the power of geomagnetic storms and that places it at the top of many scientists' most fascinating phenomena list. And that's precisely why it's #5 on ours.
- Do you agree with the aurora's #5 ranking, based on its extraordinary cause and environmental impact? Why or why not?

The *Mandans*, a Native American people living in North Dakota, said that an aurora was the glow from the fires of northern tribes boiling their enemies in huge pots!

5   4   3   2   1

(4) COMET

Comets with orbits that regularly bring them close to Earth are called "short period" comets.

WHAT IS IT? Comets can appear anywhere in the sky and are usually visible only at night.

WOW FACTOR: A comet seems to appear from nowhere, moving across the sky with a pale, glowing tail, and then seems to disappear just as mysteriously into the far reaches of the solar system.

Comets are the "dirty snowballs" or "icy mudballs" of the solar system! They hurtle through space at incredible speeds. And there could be as many as a trillion of them out there!

Although there are so many comets out there in space, we get to see a bright one only once in a decade. When comets do appear, they seem to come out of nowhere, growing brighter and brighter. A long brilliant tail trails behind. Then, in a flash, it disappears.

In early history, people didn't know what to think of this strange phenomenon. Some were afraid that these "sky serpents" had come to eat Earth and destroy humankind. Others thought comets were omens — signs of terrible events such as plagues, famines, wars, or the death of a ruler. In 44 B.C., a comet's appearance was interpreted by the Romans as an omen foretelling the assassination of Julius Caesar later that same year.

Read on to find out the source behind this fascinating astronomical phenomenon, ranked at #4 on our list ...

hurtle: *move very fast and with a lot of force*

COMET

Small comets burn away when they enter Earth's atmosphere.

WHAT ABOUT IT?

Comets are called dirty snowballs because they're really just balls of dust, dirt, and gases held together by a layer of ice. When a comet becomes visible to us, all we see is what looks to be a really large and bright ball of light. The most spectacular part of this sight is the stream of matter that trails behind the comet, forming an enormous tail. The comet flies across the sky and then disappears again.

BUT HOW?

As a comet nears the sun, the immense heat vaporizes its icy bits. A cloud of dust and gas is released that stretches for tens of thousands of miles. The particles in this cloud glow like a neon sign, reflecting light from the sun. Meanwhile, solar wind from the sun pushes the cloud away from the body of the comet — this is what gives a comet its striking tail. If the comet is traveling toward the sun, the tail will follow behind. If the comet is traveling away from the sun, the tail will be in front.

vaporizes: *turns into a gas*

Quick Fact

Some scientists believe that comet dust is left over from when the solar system was formed. This makes the dust and dirt very useful as samples of the early makeup of the solar system.

After several thousand years of orbiting the sun, comets will eventually "die." How do you think that works? Hint: Think about what it is that makes comets shine so brilliantly in our skies.

WHERE IN THE WORLD?

Comets orbit the sun far away from Earth. Sometimes one comet might crash into another. Or it might come really close to a nearby star. In either case, the comet is knocked out of its normal orbit, ends up on a path toward the sun, and begins to travel into the inner solar system, where we reside. That's when we get the chance to see this astronomical phenomenon.

The tail of a comet is tens of thousands of miles long!

The Expert Says...

" Comets are the oldest objects in the solar system, and they have been stored in almost 'deep freeze' conditions at the edge of the solar system from the time they formed 4.5 billion years ago. "

— Dan Andrews, comet expert, Open University

10   9   8   7   6

Comet Impact?

Worried about the possibility of comets striking Earth? If you are, you should read this Q&A from NASA's research center on asteroid and comet hazards ...

Q What size comets are considered dangerous?

A The Earth's atmosphere protects us from comets smaller than a modest office building. Slightly bigger comets could do some serious damage on a local scale. Much bigger ones would produce severe environmental damage on a global scale (e.g., loss of crops worldwide followed by starvation and disease). Still larger comets would cause mass extinctions, like the one that scientists believe wiped out the dinosaurs 65 million years ago.

Q What is the risk of a comet hitting Earth?

A Statistically, the greatest danger is from a mid-sized comet. On average, one of these will collide with Earth once or twice per million years, producing a global catastrophe that would kill a substantial (but unknown) fraction of Earth's human population.

catastrophe: *terrible disaster*

Q How much warning will we have?

A With undiscovered comets, there would be no warning — the first indication of a collision would be a flash of light and the shaking of the ground as they hit. That said, any comet that is going to hit Earth will swing near our planet many times before it hits. This means we would probably discover it and have a few decades' warning before it actually hits.

Q How can we protect ourselves?

A A comet impact is the only major natural hazard that we can effectively protect ourselves against by deflecting (or destroying) the object before it hits Earth. The next best thing would be to evacuate regions near the point of impact (where damage would be the greatest) and hide out in safer areas.

Quick Fact

In July 1994, large chunks of the comet Shoemaker-Levy 9 slammed into Jupiter. The explosions upon impact were a million times more powerful than the energy released by a hydrogen bomb. The resulting mushroom cloud was larger than the size of Asia!

Take Note

Auroras at #5 regularly give us amazing light shows in the night sky. Comets, on the other hand, keep even astronomers on edge. They're rare, but they have the potential to cause some very real problems for us. They're not just a pretty sight. That's why the comet comes in at #4.
- Do you think governments should invest time and money into preparing for a comet impact with Earth? Why or why not?

5   4   3   2   1

③ ROGUE WAVE

In December 2000, the "Max Wave" project
was set up to prove the existence of rogue
waves like this computer-generated one.
Two Earth-scanning satellites monitored
the oceans for three weeks.

What Do You Think?

1. Do you agree with our ranking? If you don't, try ranking them yourself. Justify your ranking with data from your own research and reasoning. You may refer to our criteria, or you may want to draw up your own list of criteria.

2. Here are three other fascinating phenomena that we considered but in the end did not include in our top 10 list: tsunamis, black holes, and ball lightning.
   • Find out more about them. Do you think they should have made our list? Give reasons for your response.
   • Are there other phenomena that you think should have made our list? Explain your choices.

Index